BLESSED!

HOW TO ATTRACT
WEALTH INTO YOUR LIFE

BLESSED!

HOW TO ATTRACT
WEALTH INTO YOUR LIFE

Best Selling Author

Dr. Shirley K. Clark

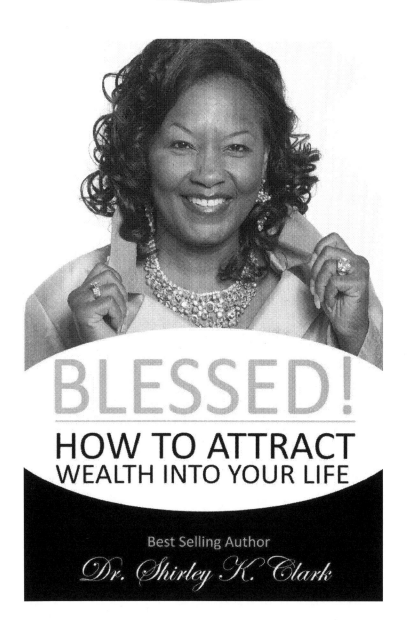

BLESSED!

HOW TO ATTRACT
WEALTH INTO YOUR LIFE

Best Selling Author

Dr. Shirley K. Clark

BLESSED! How to Attract Wealth Into Your life

Copyright © 2015
Dr. Shirley K. Clark | Shirley Clark International Ministries

Printed in the United States of America

Library of Congress – Catalogued in Publication Data

ISBN 13: 978-0692579794
ISBN 10: 0692579796

Published by:
Jabez Books Writers' Agency
(A Division of Clark's Consultant Group)
www.clarksconsultantgroup.com

Unless otherwise indicated all scriptural quotations are taken from the King James Version of the Bible.

1. Law of Attraction 2. Personal Finance 3. Entrepreneurship
4. Personal Success

Dedication

This book is dedicated to the Durham County Library System and its staff (past and present).

It was at the Durham County Library that my life began to change radically for the best. When I started working at the Durham County Library in 1982, I had very little professional work experience. I was not a reader nor did I know the value of being a lifelong learner. However, the 13 years I worked in the library system redefined and catapulted my life into realms I could only imagine at times. So when my tenure was up in the Durham County Library System, not only was I an avid reader, but I had learned and developed so much academically, professionally and intellectually.

Now, 33 years later (2015), I am a best-selling author, I have written over 22 books, and I own a Writer's Agency (which we have assisted over 70 authors in self-publishing books). I also own a PR & Marketing Firm, a Corporate Coaching & Consultant Service, and a Leadership Institute.

I know today, I could not be where I am without some incredible people that believed and supported me while I was an employee in the Durham County Library System. They made my journey there so much easier.

If you would allow me, I would like to give them homage. I would like to thank:

- **Dale Gaddis,** *Former Main Library Director*
- **Betty White,** *Former Assistant Director of the Main Library*
- **Carolyn Robinson,** *Former Supervisor, Circulation Department*
- **Sandra Roberson,** *Former Head Children's Librarian*
- **Carol Passmore,** *Former Supervisor, Project LIFT*
- **John Blake,** *Former Branch Librarian & Supervisor, Parkwood Library*
- **Mrs. White,** *Former Head Librarian, Branch Library Services*
- **Joyce McNeill,** *Former Operations Manager*
- **Anna Cromwell,** *Head, Children's Librarian*
- **The Entire Reference Department**

I pray that the rest of your life will be forever blessed as all of you have blessed my life!

More Books By

Dr. Shirley K. Clark

Pray & Grow Richer

Pray & Grow Richer Devotional Journal

Think Like A Millionaire, Be A Millionaire

Discovering Your Destiny

Birthing Your Destiny

Living Your Destiny

The Ministry of Intercession

52 Laws of Prayer

Intercessors' Insight: 40 Truths About The Ministry

of Intercession

The Power of the "IF" Prayer Manual

Endorsements

Dr. Shirley Clark is an innovative leader and a major blessing to everyone with which she connects. To know Dr. Clark is to know the "embodiment" of dynamism! She has an uncanny ability to create wealth and be a catalyst for others to grow in their purpose. This book is an extension of Dr. Clark's wisdom and knowledge. Read it! It will certainly help you move forward toward your destiny.

Dr. Teresa Hairston
Founder/President, Gospel Heritage Foundation

Your pocket book can only grow to the extent that the mind does! If you are ready to attract wealth and enjoy a life of financial freedom, here's your ticket. In this game changing book, Dr. Shirley Clark will show you how to think like a millionaire and reap the benefits of a millionaire mindset. So follow these principles, mind your business and watch it grow.

Ken Brown
International Business Coach
Bestselling Author/Entrepreneur

Dr. Shirley Clark is incredible! Since the time I have met her, she has introduced me to more millionaires and forward thinking people that I have ever met in a short period of time. This book, *"Blessed,"* is an extension of the greatness that is associated with her life. I encourage everyone to read this book if you are serious about becoming wealthy and living a financial free life.

Dorothy CooK
Millionaire Maker
Platinum President of Ardyss Int'l
Founder, Amateur Millionaire TV Show, Aired on BET

Table of Contents

THIS IS MY STORY AND I AM STICKING TO IT!

IT WAS A DAY I WOULD NEVER FORGET.
It was my high school graduation. As the great Charles Dickens's novel said, "It was the best of times and the worst of times." I was seventeen, and I was quite ignorant to all that was going on around me during this period in my life. I had very little insight about my graduation and education as a whole. All I knew was that it was expected of me

to finish high school, but completing it had no real long-term meaning in my life. You see, the entire seventeen years of my life, I was reared in an impoverished environment. My mother had only an eighth-grade education, and I don't really think she knew why I needed to finish high school, no more than it was expected of a child.

When my mother and father married, they were sixteen years old. They lived in a rural community down on the East Coast, Washington, NC. Everybody in the community mostly worked in fields planting and harvesting mostly corn, collard greens, and tobacco. Even now, I can still see myself working in tobacco barns, gathering, and tying tobacco to be placed on a pole. So when my parents married at such a young age, they had to forfeit their education to work to create a life for themselves.

A year later, their lives were challenged more as they begin having children. Every year following for four years, they had a child. After a one-year break, they had four more children. One did not live, but as you can imagine, taking care of all of us was a real challenge. But everything went from bad to worse when my father started drinking, so I was told.

Being the youngest child in the family, I don't remember these years much, but my older siblings did. They have shared with me that when my daddy would drink, occasionally, he would become so enraged that he would physically abuse my mother. This went on for years, until my mother made the decision to leave my daddy.

I was five years old when she left my daddy to try and make a better life for herself and us, so she moved back to her hometown, Durham, North Carolina. However, the biggest problem was that she had no viable working skills other than working in corn and tobacco fields. Also, when she left, she could not take us with her. Her plan was to go back home and try and make a living for herself and come back and get us.

Our caretakers during this transitional period in her life were other family members. It was three years from the time my mother dropped us off at one of her family member's house until we were able to join her as a family again. These three years were some of the darkest times in my family life. We endured so much physical and psychological abuse during these years.

But when I was finally united with my mother, I was so happy. I can remember the day like it was yesterday. I was sitting in the backseat of my uncle's car as he was taking me to be with my

I had no idea what life was going to be like when I got back with my mother, but I definitely did not expect to live in the kind of substandard living I was about to endure.

mother after those three years. The plan was to take the three youngest children first (me, my brother Jimmy, and my sister Rosa) and then on another trip take the other four (Sylvester, Elsie, Charles and Kenny).

Sitting in the backseat of the car, eight years old, all I could say over and over in my mind, "I am going home to be with my mama." So much joy was in my heart that day. Truly, I can remember it like it was yesterday, and I am now fifty-five years old. Such overwhelming joy filled my heart. But I did not know what life had in store for me. I did not know that being with someone who loved you, and you loved them back could be so bad. I had no idea what life was going to be like when I got back with my mother, but I definitely did not expect to live in the kind of substandard living I was about to endure.

Because my mother had little education, the only job she could find was being a cook at "greasy spoon" places and cafeterias. If all of our utilities were on at the same time, it was a miracle. I remember having to fill the bathtub up

When you grow up in an impoverished environment, I think it is a given having good clothes to wear would be a constant problem. So some-times I would go to school with mismatched clothes on.

with water because the water was getting ready to be cut off. For nine years, survival was our main focus.

From day to day, we did not know how we were going to make it. My mother would cook a whole bag of rice just to feed us. Beans (Great Northern, pinto, black-eyed pea) were a stapled food in our house. Anything that would expand and increase, my mother cooked it. The favorite thing we loved for our mother to cook was homemade biscuits. She could cook some biscuits. They would be so soft and evenly brown on the top and bottom. Life was always about making it through the day, and the days were extremely long especially during the school year for me.

When you grow up in an impoverished environment, I think it is a given having good clothes to wear would be a constant problem. So sometimes I would go to school with mismatched clothes on. Of course, wearing garments like this to school often caused you to be the joke of the class. When this would happen to me, I would play it off, but I would be dying inside. I often tell people my self-esteem was so low by the time I was an adult that I did not know how to be "normal"—whatever that means.

Life growing up in poverty was awful! The fear of being laughed at in school dangled over my head every day of my life during the school year. But I got through each year, passing from one grade to another until I reached the twelfth grade. Oh, and by the way, I had only one sibling that finished high school prior to this, and that was my sister Rosa; she was two years ahead of me. All my other brothers and sisters (five) dropped out of high school.

In my twelfth grade, I was looking forward to graduating like my sister Rosa. We were somewhat close, but because she was two years older than me, she was blessed to have friends in our neighborhood, whereby their parents were educated and they had a better lifestyle than us. We know today this saved my sister from being a high school dropout because they gave her a vision for what life could be like if she finished high school and perhaps go to college.

Unfortunately, I did not have friends like this, so survival was still my mind-set. So going to school was what I supposed to do, but I really didn't know why I needed to go to school. I had no one in my life to bring clarity to this matter. The world was such a mystery to me.

Entering the last year of high school, I was just trying to survive. However, I had started working, so I was able to buy a few pieces of garments that were appropriate for school. I felt good about this, however, the twelfth grade was "no piece of cake." What I realized after flunking the first semester in English, I had to pass the second semester to

> *After starting the class, I felt like I had gotten out of the frying pan and into the fire when the teacher began to teach the class. I knew immediately I was in trouble.*

graduate from high school. I never thought about how important English was until I was faced with this dilemma.

I took a creative writing course the second semester, hoping this would be easy, and I would pass the class with no problem. After starting the class, I felt like I had gotten out of the frying pan and into the fire when the teacher began to teach the class. I knew immediately I was in trouble. I was not sure what this class was going to be like, but certainly, I had no idea I would be writing stories.

This class was a nightmare! My mind could not put a subject and a verb together, nor did I have an understanding of punctuation. I did not know how to construct or stop a sentence. I really worked hard to try and make sense out of writing, but all I knew how to write was a run-on sentence. I had to pass this class in order to graduate from high school.

I don't think I ever made a passing grade on any of my writings in this class. But I worked hard intentionally to make sure I did all the homework that were required. However, no matter how hard

I worked, English just didn't make sense to me. The whole while I was struggling in this class, not graduating from high school was constantly dangling over my head. I felt so ashamed and embarrassed. I wanted to fix it, but I felt powerless. I told no one.

So when the semester ended, which was the end of the school year, I did not know what to do. I was scared, and I definitely did not want to see my grade because I did not want to see that I had failed. Because if I did, this meant facing up to another truth: I will not be graduating, which I knew I was not capable of doing. My solution: never ask the teacher if I passed or not. To this day, I never knew my final grade in this class.

However, the hardest thing for me was going through the motion with my mother and sister acting as though I knew for sure I was going to graduate. Somehow my mother scraped up enough money to pay for my cap and grown, so everything was taken care of for my graduation. All the while this was going on, I was being haunted by the fact; I might not graduate.

The school year ended, and graduation day arrived. I was "one scared chick." All day long, internally I was in turmoil. I am sure I had created some story just in case my name was not called, so as my mother and my sister Rosa sat on the bleachers with me, I was praying hard inside.

When it was our time for our row to line up to receive our high school diploma, I got in line with everyone else. When I reached the stage and they called my name, while I wanted to be joyful, all I could feel was relief. So I plastered a smile on

Even though I had received my diploma, I still felt like an imposter. I was so guilt-written that I never really experienced the joy of that day. I knew what was going on. It was the fact that I had a secret, and I was too embarrassed to tell anyone. I did not want to be a failure.

my face and went back to my seat and hugged my mother and sister. Even though I had received my diploma, I still felt like an imposter. I was so guilt-written that I never really experienced the joy of that day. I knew what was going on. It was the fact that I had a secret, and I was too embarrassed to tell anyone. I did not want to be a failure.

This was such a conflict in my heart that I kept this secret for about twenty-eight years before I was able to share it with anyone. But when I did, it was a period in my life where I could celebrate what I had come through. You see, by the time I shared my story, I was then an owner of a writer's agency, *Jabez Books*, and had helped over 70 other authors write and publish their books. Also, in the first five years of establishing my Agency, I published and copyrighted personally over eight books. As of 2014, I have written and published over 21 books.

When I think about my life and what I went through and where I am now, I realized my main debilitating problem was my environment. Was it nature or nurture? For me, it was nature—the environment I grew up in, and because of this, this environment defined and hindered my learning process. When you have a survival mind-set as a child, your focus and thoughts are on just making it day by day, especially when your parents have little education and they really don't know the impact of being educated. This was my situation. Because my mother had little education, she could not mentor me in this area. All she knew, I was supposed to go to school.

But I thank God today for His restoring grace. He restored to me the years that the cankerworm and palmerworm stole from me according to Joel 2 in the Bible. We can be restored no matter what we have gone through to hinder our progress.

My biggest change came in my life when I got a job working for the library system in Durham, NC. Surrounded by books, I began to realize how important is was for me to read. I was a part of the Circulation Department, and one day, this became solidified in my heart. I heard in my spirit: "Why do you think all these people are checking out all these books? It must be something to books." All the "bells and whistles" went off inside me. I immediately started checking out twenty-five to thirty books at a time. I had a thirst to read that could not be quenched.

I try to drive and read. Every break or lunch I got, I read books. I read all types of books: fiction and nonfiction (cooking, personal finance, self-help, organization, motivational, mystery, etc.). It was amazing what I found out in books. I felt like I had tapped into a resource that was never ending. To this day, I am an avid reader.

So not only do we own a Writer's Agency, but we also have five other departments under our consultant group. We have a PR and marketing firm, a management and entertainment service, a leadership institute, an event planning department, and a corporate training and coaching service.

And because of all the things I have now done, and all the people I have met, I am convinced more than ever that the sky is no

> *Because of all the things the Lord has allowed me to do and all the people He has allowed me to meet, I am convinced more than ever that the sky is no longer the limit for me. The universe is my goal and my classroom. Every day I wake up, I go to school.*

longer the limit for me. The universe is my goal and my classroom. Every day I wake up, I go to school.

There are things I have never seen, and there are things I don't know. Therefore, I cannot afford to waste moments in my life. There are people who say things like, "Child, I am just killing time or wasting time." Two things I don't do: I don't kill time, nor do I waste time. Time is something we can never get back. We have to be productive citizens on this earth and maximize our existence.

What do you want to do in life? What do you want to be in life? Whatever your answers to these questions, I want you to know, you have no limitations. All you have is an access problem.

As I conclude this section, I want you to know that for you to thrive on this earth, you have to take on the mind-set of a global solutionist. While there might be a problem, there is a solution for the problem.

I have a book out that I am on tour with that is called, "Pray & Grow Richer." For four years, I seek and soaked in the presence of God for about 80% of my time. I limited my comings and goings because I wanted a change in my financial portfolio. I read only books by millionaires, and I did numerous things to provoke increase in my life.

In four years, my income increased three times, created business ideas were stimulated, and I was self-taught in how to do graphic design and all types of technical programs. It was phenomenal! This year, we are preparing for the overflow even the more. We have already hired contract service providers to assist us with our anticipated growth this year (2015), and we will be expanding the business also.

We expect this to be a banner year for us and our company. We are big thinkers because we know, no matter where you begin in life is certainly not the end of the matter. So many people are prisoners to their past, but they don't have to be. You can create the world you desire by being the change you want to see. If you don't know how to do it, read up on it. If you don't know who to talk to, read up on it. If you don't know how to get the money you need, read up on it. Reading is an empowerment tool.

When I was writing my book, Pray & Grow Richer, I was led to write a whole chapter about reading; it is called, *"The Empowered Mind."* Here is an excerpt out of this chapter:

It is said that in five years you will be the same person, except for the CDs you listen to, the DVDs you watch, the books you read, and the people you hang around. If you want your world to change, you have to start reading TODAY!

It is also said: "If you read thirty to sixty minutes a day in a subject of your choice, after three years you will be known in your community, five years you will be known across the country, and after seven years, you will have worldwide recognition." Listen, if you are not a reader, you need to stop what you are doing and pray to have the passion and the desire to read.

Reading is extremely important to your mental, physical, emotional, and financial makeup. According to Myron Golden in his book, From Trash Man to Cash Man, *"Rich people educate themselves, and poor people entertain themselves."* This statement alone should provoke you to read if you are not a reader and having financial problems.

Reading provides greater avenues or more opportunities for God to expand your sphere of influence and financial portfolio.

Reading brings about expansion,
and expansion brings about exposure.

I challenge you to wake up every morning expecting the universe to be in your favor. You are well able to abound, and there is nothing impossible for you to overcome. You are enough. You are smart enough. You are wise enough. You are clever

> *Wake up every morning expecting the universe to be in your favor.*

enough. You are resourceful enough. You have enough ideas to pull off miracles. You are amazing!

Now, let me encourage you to position yourself for change. Make a conscious decision as you read each step in this book that you are going to activate what you are reading. You need to tell yourself that you are no longer going to be the same or struggling for the rest of your life. Say this with me.....*THE STRUGGLE IS OVER!*

Say it again.......

THE STRUGGLE IS OVER!

If you will take on *the struggle is over* mindset when you read this book, I believe you will fare better when you finish reading this book.

See you at the top!!!

And never stop stretching and growing!

Step 1

UNDERSTAND YOUR BELIEF SYSTEM AND ASSESS YOUR LIFE

ONE OF THE HARDEST THINGS THAT I have noticed with most people when it comes to finance, debt and money is that they have a hard time being honest about their condition and situation. I am especially aware of this when I interact with people that we say, "have the gift of gab," because often these types of people have a tendency to try and over talk their situation or minimize the actual depth or severity of their circumstance. As well, they always have some way of legitimizing their predicament instead of facing the truth.

> *For you to be successful in life financially, you have to face the truth about your finances. You have to tell yourself the truth.*

For you to be successful in life financially, you have to face the truth about your finances. *You have to tell yourself the truth*. You cannot properly assess where you need to go, what you need to do until you are honest about your financial state. Then and only then will you be able to determine the steps you would need to take to reach your desired goal in life regarding wealth, success and being financially free.

Now, to help facilitate this process, here is a checklist of questions to consider:

- ✓ *Do I believe I can be rich?*
- ✓ *Do I despise wealthy people?*
- ✓ *Do I talk more about what I don't have than what I have or want to have?*
- ✓ *Do I believe that riches and wealth are for certain people, but not me?*
- ✓ *Do I believe people with money are evil?*

- ✓ *Do I believe more in being financially secure than financially free?*

- ✓ *Do I believe that rich people will go to hell?*

- ✓ *Do I truly believe in tithes, offerings and giving?*

- ✓ *Do I truly believe that God wants me wealthy?*

- ✓ *Do I do things that reinforce poverty or lack?*

- ✓ *Do most or all of my friends have money struggles?*

- ✓ *Do I believe I will always have a car payment or house note?*

✓ *Do I teach my children (if you have any) that money doesn't grow on trees?*

✓ *Do I believe that I will never be wealthy?*

If you believe any of these statements, then you have some work to do. However, I have good news, you are not alone. Most people have a poverty mentality or have grown up in a household that modeled or taught **WRONG** money management principles to them. This was my scenario. Because I grew up in gross poverty, I was not only broke, but I had a poverty mentality. So I had to dislodge all of this information and cultural experience in order for me to be successful.

You have to do the same if you were reared in this type of environment as well!

As I said earlier, the hardest thing for some people to do is tell the truth about where they are or how they got into a certain bad situation. I believe, one of the main reasons some people do this is that they want to look prosperous more than what they really are.

In 2015, I launched a Financial Empowerment Challenge Certification program called, *Pray & Grow Richer 90 Day Financial Empowerment Challenge.* We had been offering this Challenge for about two years prior to this, but it was not as impactful as I wanted it to be with some of the participants. I realized after two years of administering this Challenge with over 100 people, because we had no set schedule to read certain material by or no real accountability markers, they did things somewhat at their comfort level or when it was convenient. By them doing this, I did not have as many success stories, at least not at the level I wanted in 90 days. You see, I knew it would work, if they worked it.

For me, this was my life. And if I was going to invest 90 days of my time with a group of people, I wanted to make a significant difference in their lives. I wanted to make more of an impact in their lives. What did I do? I had to assess my process. What I realized, I did not give them any deadlines, markers or goals to work toward throughout the Challenge. And just in case you are wondering what this 90 Day Financial Empowerment Challenge is then let me share with you about the Challenge.

*Our **American Dream** became an **American Nightmare!** I found out everything we were taught to strive for in society to become a middle class family came with such a high price.*

About seven years ago (2008), I decided I had enough of my family living from paycheck to paycheck. Even though looking at our situation, my husband and I, it looked like we had the *American Dream,* and we did by society's standard. But this is what the American dream **blessed** us with: a house with a mortgage; a car with a car payment; two children: a girl and a boy, and I might say, they were great kids, but we still had to take care of them; 401K and other retirement and insurance plans; and consumer debt totaling up to about $80,000. So our *American Dream* became an *American Nightmare!* I found out everything we were taught to strive for in society to become a middle class family came with such a high price.

The credit card issuers were calling us constantly. For about a year, when my husband was laid off from work, we could not make all the payments that were required on time, so our phone would ring all the time. At times, I had to take the phone off the hook just to keep the phone from ringing so much. However, we were always with some type of income, it was just not at the level we had grown accustomed to, so somebody did not get paid, and most of the time, it was the credit card companies.

We consulted with an attorney through our prepaid legal service, and they instructed us to file bankruptcy. However, this did not set well with me. I had friends who had done this, and I just did not want to go through this process. If not this, then what were we going to do?

There is a story in the Bible about a King called Jehoshaphat in 2 Chronicles, Chapter 20. It is an incredible story about how this king found himself surrounded by his enemies who wanted to fight him. When Jehoshaphat heard what was going on, he saw no natural way out, no way of winning the battle. But the thing that stood out in this story is what Jehoshaphat did and declared. Here are some excerpts from the story:

> *[1]It came to pass after this also, that the children of Moab, and the children of Ammon, and with them other beside the Ammonites, came against Jehoshaphat to battle.*

*² Then there came some that told Jehoshaphat, saying, There cometh **a great multitude** against thee from beyond the sea on this side Syria; and, behold, they be in Hazazontamar, which is Engedi.*

*³ And Jehoshaphat **feared, and set himself to seek the LORD, and proclaimed a fast** throughout all Judah.*

*⁴ And Judah gathered themselves together, **to ask help of the LORD:** even out of all the cities of Judah **they came to seek the LORD.***

Then it said, Jehoshaphat prayed.

*¹² O our God, wilt thou not judge them? **FOR WE HAVE NO MIGHT AGAINST THIS GREAT COMPANY THAT COMETH AGAINST US;***

NEITHER KNOW WE WHAT TO DO: BUT OUR EYES ARE UPON THEE...

¹⁸ And Jehoshaphat bowed his head with his face to the ground: and all Judah and the inhabitants of Jerusalem fell before the LORD, worshipping the LORD...

²² And when they began to sing and to praise, the LORD set ambushments against the children of Ammon, Moab, and mount Seir, which were come against Judah; and they were smitten...

²⁵ And when Jehoshaphat and his people came to take away the spoil of them, they found among them in abundance both riches with the dead bodies, and precious jewels, which they stripped off for themselves, more than they could carry away: and they were three days in gathering of the spoil, it was so much.

When Jehoshaphat said, "... *for we have no might against this great company that cometh against us; neither know we what to do: but our eyes are upon thee,"* this is the way I felt when all the credit card companies were haunting us. I felt like a great company was coming out against us. And let me clarify something here. We did not run up $80,000 worth of consumer debt. Quite a bit of this were penalties, late fees, transfer fees, annual fees and all other fees the credit card companies and the banking system **ensnare** us with. So when we were in this predicament, I was reminded of this story. So I did what Jehoshaphat did. I prayed and I sought God.

I said, *"Lord, I don't know what to do or how we are going to get out of this situation, but my eyes are upon you."* I put together a strategic plan to do one thing for as long as I needed to and that was to seek God, soak, meditate, and to strengthen my relationship with money.

I learned a long time ago, if there is a testimony of someone surviving a similar situation that I was now going through, then I knew for a surety, I could be a candidate for this same type of blessing – for this same type of miracle.

I learned a long time ago, if there is a

testimony of someone surviving a similar situation that I was now going through, then I knew for a surety, I could be a candidate for this same type of blessing – for this same type of miracle.

So for over four years, I sought and soaked (meditated) in the presence of God regarding our financial situation, but it only took two years for us to pay off our consumer credit card debt. We got rid of all our credit cards and we paid cash for everything. At the end of four years, my personal and business income had increased three times.

One of the first things I did at the beginning of my seeking was that I went through a 90 day financial empowerment exercise. There were eight things that I heard and read about in a book and on a CD that multi-millionaires said they did to launch their financial increase. Well, I thought, if they did it, and it worked, I had nothing to lose.

It was quite a challenge doing these eight things *every day for 90 day*, but I wanted to prove these multi-millionaires to be wrong. *But then I thought, what if it does work,* They promised pretty much if anyone did these things, their financial and/or life situation would change significantly or for the better.

Well, I had nothing to lose and everything to gain!

Now, almost seven years later, my income has increased over five times; I drive a S Class 550 Mercedes Benz (an $80,000 car), which was given to me; I have now employed in our business four staff members and several contract individuals. I now have a ministry office in Holland, Texas, North Carolina and another one pending in London; and in a year or so, we are hoping to open several businesses. And to put the "icing on the cake," my daughter is in her second year of medical school.

What happened in my life or to my life....well, I believe it was best said in the story about Jehoshaphat.

> *And when Jehoshaphat and his people came to take away the spoil of them, **they found among them in abundance both riches with the dead bodies, and precious jewels, which they stripped off for themselves, more than they could***

carry away: and they were three days in gathering of the spoil, it was so much.

Jehoshaphat and his people were **blessed** tremendously with precious jewels and money. They were so **blessed** that it took three days for them to collect all the spoils that was left behind. In fact, I had a similar occurrence in a meeting like this in Maryland in America. As I was hosting one of our Pray & Grow Richer Tours in this state, a woman attending the meeting **blessed** me with $2400 worth of jewelry and fashion. It was such an overwhelming blessing.

I was so grateful and I will forever remember this lady. Almost every time I wear any of the pieces she gave me, I receive compliments. I came home with a whole carrying cart full of jewelry (necklaces, watches, bracelets, purses, rings, you name it).

So what I saw happened in my life; I wanted it to happen in other people's lives. This is why I started the 90 Day Financial Empowerment Challenge. I wanted to become an advocate for

Even though I knew it would be a difficult challenge for most, even though the steps were easy, but it would require a whole lot of discipline. But I knew it would be worth it.

other people's change and financial empowerment. Also, there were so many incredible byproducts that manifested in my life because of what I did that I knew if I could get a group of people thinking right or on the right path, they will have a better or higher chance of making it in life. Even though I knew it would be a difficult challenge for most, even though the steps were easy, but it would require a whole lot of discipline. But I knew it would be worth it.

Going through the Challenge, I knew the participants would better understand the system which so many of us had been "sucked" into and why. They would also understand the need to forgive themselves for past behaviors and failures, and that many of them had no control over in this consumer craving vacuum society. They would learn that we were all at the mercy of the systems of this world, and the reality is, we were all "hoodwinked." And after we have been hoodwinked (made into these consumers driven over-indulgence individuals), then they would punish us by giving us bad credit scores, and ultimately boycotting us from getting any other loans, services, or products whereby we cannot create a better life for us and our families.

When I think about this, I think it is best said in a movie I love, *"Ever After: A Cinderella Story,"* by the main character, Drew Barrymore who played Cinderella.

There was a key segment in the movie that Drew Barrymore (Cinderella) was trying to buy a man back that used to be a servant in her home that was held captive in the king's palace and the servant was getting ready to be shipped off to be sold as a slave. His wife was still a servant in her home and she loved them dearly, and she wanted to have this woman's husband returned to her.

When she told the prison keeper or guard she wanted to buy him back with the money she had, he scoffed at the amount she was offering. Becoming a little upset, she demanded that they release him. Then the prison keeper became enraged and began shouting at her. Just as he did this, the prince arrived on the scene and reprimanded him for raising his voice to a lady. He backed down and apologized to the prince and then he said he was only following orders and was taking these slaves to where he was instructed to take them.

Then Drew Barrymore (Cinderella) said, "A servant is not a slave your highness." And the prince said, "Do tell." This is what she said,

> *"If you suffer your people to be ill-educated and to have their manners corrupt from infancy, then punish them for which their first education exposed them. Whatever to be concluded that*

you first make thieves and then you punish them."

This is a powerful statement in the movie and the prince was truly touched by it. After hearing this, the prince instructed the guard to release the man.

But this is what the credit card industry and lending institutions have done to so many people in society. They have ill-educated us and corrupted us from our infancy to their systems, then they punish us for what our first education exposed us to *from them.* The amount of credit card applications we get in the mail and commercials we see about get this or that card to be able to do the things you want to do in life is ridiculous. Some even have the audacity to say things like, *"Be free to do whatever you want to do in life."* What a high price for freedom?

As of October 2015, the Nell Wallet blog website reported these statistics:

U.S. household consumer debt profile:

- Average credit card debt: **$16,140**
- Average mortgage debt: **$155,361**
- Average student loan debt: **$31,946**

In total, American consumers owe:

- $11.85 trillion in debt

  ......An increase of 1.7% from last year

- $890.9 billion in credit card debt
- $8.17 trillion in mortgages
- $1.19 trillion in student loans

  ......An increase of 7.1% from last year

(https://www.nerdwallet.com/blog/credit-card-data/average-credit-card-debt-household/)

These statistics are astounding. You have to ask yourself, how could this be? How can so many **educated** people (college graduates) find themselves in this predicament? I will tell you how, *through ill-education and misinformation.*

We, people in society, made the mistake to believe that those that control the lending institutions were for us, but in actuality, they were not. When you borrow money from a lending institution, they charge you more interest than they pay you when you lend your money to them. Whether it is a money market fund, CD or any other investment opportunity, we always get paid less when they are using our money. I like the question one of the wealth coaches I know asks in her coaching sessions, "Why is their money more important than our money."

The answer to the question is, it is not. But since they are the "Big Dog" holding the upper hand they often are the policies and decision makers. Bottom line: They pay you *less* to use your money. And here is the "kicker." They invest your money, so they are making even more money off your money.

These statistics clearly prove my claim. Sure, we have an over-indulgenced undisciplined amount of people in society, but the making of this sect of people was formed within the systems of this world. The ill-education and corruption from infancy that we were predisposed to regarding wealth and being financially free.

What do we need to do? We have to become smarter producers and not consumers. We have to strive daily and relentlessly to get this nature of consumerism out of our system and psyche. We are called to produce wealth not spend money!

> *But remember the LORD your God, because he is the one who gives you the* **ABILITY TO PRODUCE WEALTH,** *in order to confirm his covenant that he promised by an oath to your ancestors, as is the case today.*
>
> *Deuteronomy 8:18*

So this is one of the first things we teach our students going through our Pray & Grow Richer 90 Day Financial Empowerment Certification Program. We teach them, they are no longer subject to this world. We want them to know

> *This is one of the first things we teach our students going through our Pray & Grow Richer 90 Day Financial Empowerment Certification Program. We teach them, they are no longer subject to this world.*

immediately, they will be in the fight of their lives to uneducate **all** that they have learned **all** their lives about money, lending institutions, formal education, and the systems of this world.

When we started the certification program this year (2015) for the first time, we had close to 100 people who registered. But just a little over 50 people actually participated, and only about 35 participants completed the program.

We really had an incredible time training and walking with this group of eager learners. We had all types of people going through the program. We had community leaders, psalmists, pastors, entrepreneurs, authors, business owners, prayer leaders, coaches, fashion designers and licensed counselors. They were from seven states in the United States: Virginia, Texas, Oklahoma, Georgia,

Maryland, North Carolina, and New York. It was an array of stellar participants.

To begin the Challenge, I knew if I was going to have a breakthrough in anyway with these participants, I knew they had to be honest with themselves. So one of the first things they had to do was submit to me an assessment of their financial situation. What I wanted to see was

What I have concluded that there is a system (visible and invisible) in this world that "compels" people to do things beyond their means. It is a faulty system, and it is a system designed to keep us broke.

what the students were up against and I also wanted to make sure they tell themselves the truth. Often people hide their true financial state in obscurity, hoping that it would somehow go away, so they don't have to deal with it or tell themselves the truth. By having them write it out, I knew there would be a level of freedom that would come into their lives that would give them a voice to their own frustration, and encourage them to press even harder to do something about it. Plus, I was there to help give them strategies to get them to their next level.

Years ago, when I met people who were always making excuses for the financial ruin, I thought they were just operating in pride. But now that I am a little older and have experienced some things in life, I have a different understanding regarding this. What I have concluded and what I have just said previously is that there is a system (visible and invisible) in this world that "compels" people to do things beyond their means. This system is a faulty system, and it is a system designed to keep us broke.

If you go along with the status quo or systems of this world, you will never be successful or be financially independent. Wealth basically comes to those who choose to believe different and do something different.

You see, when you choose to believe different, to challenge your belief system, it will truly be an uphill battle. The environment most of us have been reared in have programmed our minds (conscious and subconscious) that this is the only way that you can thrive or it is the only system we have "permission" to work within. And if you dare to venture out beyond this system, you will fail. THIS IS A LIE!

Author, Dr. Walter Fletcher wrote a book, titled, "**Recovering the Soul**, and it says, *"To a certain* *degree we are all shaped by the cultural norms and values in which we are born. This may be a good thing, or it may be a hard shell we have to break out of in order to find our own identity and purpose."* For many of us, it is the latter. It is a hard shell to break free from. But regardless, it can be done.

> *There is another system you can get your cues from and redefine your life's script, but first, you need to know, you can be blessed, and be financially independent.*

There is another system you can get your cues from and redefine your life's script, but first, you need to know, you can be blessed, and be financially independent. I like what Ken Brown says, the first youngest African-American owner of a McDonald's franchise, he says success also leaves clues. Any thought or mindset that tells you different, you have to abandon it. You have to fight with all of your might to block any debilitating thoughts that threaten your success.

If your daddy or mommy was an alcoholic, let alcohol know, it is not going to work for your life. If your siblings were drug addicts, let drugs know, it is not going to work for you. They are not welcome and they are detractors from you getting to your wealthy place. And when you get there, they will still not be a part of your life. We have to renew our minds and create a new system of beliefs that only mirror success and prosperity.

Write the Vision

Years ago when I was working in corporate America, I was only making about $22,000 a year. And in 1995, I knew I could not continue to live like this. I just felt, I was made for more. I can't explain it, I just knew what I was doing and where I was in life financially were not my destiny.

Around the beginning of the year, I attended a workshop at the Durham County Library, and the presenter was training the participants on how to design a "mission statement" for their entire life. Now, when I thought about a life's mission statement, I was thinking probably the way you are thinking. A five to six line paragraph emphasizing your passion and calling in life. However, this was not what this workshop was about. It was about assessing your life, being true to what you really wanted to accomplish in life, formulating timelines and deadlines to achieve these things, listing the tools or the resources you will need to accomplish these things, as well as justifying or giving yourself legitimate reasons why you wanted to do these things and what you will do when you get each of these goals and objectives completed. It was awesome!

That night after the workshop, I knew I had to do this for my life. I needed a guidepost out of my situation, and I wanted it NOW! At this point in my life, I am not sure when I started working on my life's mission statement, but I am sure it was almost immediately. I do recall working on it during my lunch hours and when I had breaks at work. I had no idea what this was going to do for my life and where it was going to take me, but I knew deep within me this was somewhat an answer to my prayers, so I did. There is an adage that says, "If you don't know where you are going in life, then you won't know when you get there."

As I am writing this book, now 20 years later, about this period in my life, I can still feel all the emotions of my desperation I was going through internally during this time. This was such a tempestuous period in my life. I was having marital problems; I was working a low paying job, and I was being falsely accused of things that affected my character by a group of people in my personal life. I was under so much stress that I would be awakened at night in bed feeling like the marrow in my bones was on fire. I would just rub and rub my leg trying to get release. Eventually, it would subside, but this went on for months. After writing my life's mission statement, immediately, I began to feel better overall. It was something about knowing more specifically what I wanted to do with my life. It was about being able to see more clearly. It was about having a written vision to gaze upon.

In the Bible in Habakkuk 2:1-3 (Amplified Version) it says:

> ¹*I will stand at my guard post And station myself on the tower; And I will keep watch to see what He will say to me, And what answer I will give [as His spokesman] when I am reproved.*

> ²*Then the LORD answered me and said, "Write the vision And engrave it plainly on [clay] tablets. So that the one who reads it will run.*

[3] "For the vision is yet for the appointed [future] time It hurries toward the goal [of fulfillment]; it will not fail. Even though it delays, wait [patiently] for it, Because it will certainly come; it will not delay.

As I was designing my life's mission statement, this scripture came to my mind. So when I completed the writing process, I decided to activate these passages of scriptures over my life's mission statement.

I would meditate, ponder and pray over my life's mission statement constantly (in my personal seeking time and throughout the day). I kept it forefronted in my mind. What was I doing, I was guarding my vision – *"I will stand at my guard post And station myself on the tower; And I will keep watch to see what He will say to me..."* -- I was keeping watch to see what I would hear during this time of seeking.

I didn't know really what to expect, but I knew I had to go into this time of seeking with an expectation that something was going to change in my situation.

I didn't know really what to expect, but I knew I had to go into this time of seeking with an expectation that something was going to change in my situation. I had a clear vision and I was prepared to do whatever I heard and/or felt that I was prompted to do – "… "*Write the vision and engrave it plainly on [clay] tablets. So that the one who reads it will run.*" This is what I was preparing to do, to run with it.

Well, to my amazement, it did not take long for my dream to come to pass. In fact, it only took three months. One of the main things I had on my life's mission statement was that I wanted to be a stay at home wife and mother – and in three months, I was a full-time homemaker. How did this come about?

Well, one day my husband received a call from a corporate executive who wanted to recruit him to work for their company. This was a job that my husband did not apply for, and he was told that someone he knew (he told him the name of the person) recommended him for the job.

When my husband told me about it, I was thrilled because I felt this was the key to me getting what I was believing for. However, my husband turned the job down. Let me say this, I never told anyone what I was believing for not even my husband. I like testimonies that are free from humans' inventions, so I told no one. Of course, I was saddened by this, but I continued my daily ritual of seeking and believing.

Also, the corporate executive did the same. He was persistent in trying to recruit my husband to work for their company, but my husband said no, again. Then finally he came back to him and said, "What will it take for you to come and work for our company?" My husband thought about it a day or so, submitted his demands, they accepted them, and in three months, I was no longer working; I was a full-time homemaker.

The amount of money that my husband asked for matched his current salary and almost mine. And since I was going to be at home, there was no need for childcare and all the other expenses we were putting out while I was working. When I saw this happened, I knew I was on to something. I kept seeking and soaking until everything on my list came to pass.

So the first step in this process of getting out of your situation is to understand your belief system and assess your current livelihood. Be honest with yourself and don't make any excuses. I have a dear friend named Tawana Williams and she was born with no arms. In spite of this, Tawana is married, has a child, is a motivational speaker & coach, author and a business woman. Tawana said her mother and grandmother, when she was growing up, would not allow her to make excuses for what she could or could not do. In fact, she said her grandmother when she tried to feel sorry for herself one day, told her, "T (is what they called her), if God would have wanted you to have arms, then He would have given them to you, so stop it and get moving."

Tawana does everything with her feet. She is incredible!

Pictures used by Permission

Also, Tawana has written a book called, *"UNarmed But Dangerous."* Here is a picture of the cover of her book. Let me encourage you to buy this book and support Tawana.

About Tawana Williams

*Tawana Williams is "The Hope Coach," who teaches others around the world how to live a life with "No More Excuses." Her dreams are to create and host her own TV Talk Show, Produce her Motivational Reality Show and to be an Executive Producer of her Debut Movie **"UNarmed But Dangerous."** Tawana's been featured on Jerry Springer sharing her story of beating the odds. Judge Hatchett as a mentor to a troubled teen, The WORD Network (twice), Manna Express TV, TCT-TV three times, The Balancing Act on Lifetime TV, The 700 Club/CBN, TBN Network, and other national/regional* *programs. Also, Tawana's story has been featured in numerous national and international magazines and has been interviewed twice by Oprah Winfrey's Producers by telephone.*

To contact or book Tawana, please visit her website at:
www.tawanawilliams.com

See, you are either going to make excuses or make money, but you won't do both.

So, let's make money!

Rich people

take responsibility

for their choices;

Poor people

make excuses.

Step 2

DECIDE THAT YOU WANT TO BE FINANCIALLY FREE

DO YOU KNOW THERE ARE PEOPLE IN society that are afraid of making decisions? They are so afraid that they never make any solid decisions at all. But if you are going to be wealthy, you can't be indecisive. You have to be someone who is not afraid of making decisions. It is called leadership or being a good leader.

Success is always attained from being focused or having clearly defined objectives. So you having the inability to make decisions, you are by default allowing other people to create your world.

> *Success is always attained from being focused or having clearly defined objectives.*

You see, everything you do will reinforce your decision(s) or lack of decision(s). This is especially true with your behavior because your behavior is designed to follow decisions you have made in your mind. This is why you have to have a "captive" mind. A mind that is guarded and secured from unwanted detractors and thoughts.

Once you have a captive mind, make a decision that you are going to be wealthy. You are going to be financially free. Don't try to figure it out, how it is going to happen, just make a quality decision that from that day forward, you are going to be wealthy.

When you make this decision, you have just told the universe to help you get there. So the following weeks and months, you have to fight with everything within you against your present reality versus your future destiny. Especially watch the words you speak and your thoughts. Don't allow you mind to wonder and feed off of the old information of past experiences. If you don't do this, you will not succeed or obtain your goal in life.

I like to think of this transitional time or period in your life like being on high alert of intruders in a homeland situation. Your homeland security within you needs to be on high alert. You are constantly watching and self-monitoring your thoughts and actions. Everything you do are building blocks based on your decisions. Fortify your mind and become tenacious about protecting the borders of your mind.

This is one area I really had to master in my life —

making decisions. Because I had been on the "low

end of the pole" so long, my self-image and self-

esteem were so low as well. Of course, I had limited

information and limited knowledge to reference in

my mind because I had been in a survival mode

since my childhood. What encouraged me as I grew

older was that people of authority and influence

started to want me in their equation and/or wanted

me on their boards or in their organizations. Over

time, I realized, I really did have something to say

and that I can "bring a lot to the table these days."

My confidence built up and I began to see my value.

Of course, I continued my lifelong learning personal development journey by continuing to read books on leadership, self-help, personal finance, empowerment, relationship, etc. until now, I am a marketplace leader, CEO of a business, community advocate, global prayer network strategist, elder in my church, board member for several non-profit organizations, founder and

> *When people ask me to make a decision about something, I do. I am very decisive; I don't mind making decisions. Leaders have to be individuals who can make decisions.*

chancellor of a leadership institute and a lot of other leadership opportunities.

Now, when people ask me to make a decision about something, I do. I am very decisive; I don't mind making decisions. Leaders have to be individuals who can make decisions. It is an inept leader that cannot make decisions.

Success follows direction. Like Ken Brown said, *"Success leaves clues."* I believe a person who does not know how to make great decisions is a person that will always be broke. They will always be at the mercy of someone else. Make a decision today that you are the creator of your own destiny, and you make power moves and decisions to reinforce your goals in life.

What is a decision? By definition a decision is a conclusion or resolution reached after consideration. Synonyms of this word is resolution, conclusion, settlement, commitment, resolve and determination. So a decision in layman's terms is a finishing, establishing component. It provides direction and a clear focus for all involved.

Leaders are decision makers. So start today leading your life towards your success destiny by making decisions that mirror your desired result.

Rich people value financial freedom; Poor people value financial security.

Step 3

THINK LIKE A MILLIONAIRE

A MIND THAT IS RULED BY SUCCESS principles will be a mind that will create and cultivate wealth in a life. If we want to be wealthy, then we have to think like rich people. If we want to be financially free, then we have to think like millionaires. Our minds are incredible.

Daily, it is said that we have 50,000 to 70,000 thoughts that run through our mind, and whatever belief system we believe in, reinforcing it will definitely not be a problem.

If your belief system is lack and poverty, and you think you will never make it, then your mind will concur with you. In fact, this is called "confirmation bias." And any thought, view or opinion that contradicts or threatens this belief system, your confirmation bias

If your belief system is lack and poverty, and you think you will never make it, then your mind will concur with you. In fact, this is called "confirmation bias."

(that which you already believe) will fight for its existence. Always remember, your mind will seek out information that matches its current belief system or bias. It is the law of confirmation bias.

So…….how do we think like a millionaire or acquire a millionaire mind? Read materials by millionaires/wealthy people or hang around wealthy people!

The quickest way to get rid of a poverty mentality is reading contradictory information **consistently.** The Bible says we should **renew** our minds, not **remove** our minds. As a Christian and a licensed minister, this is a pervasive problem in the church community as a whole. While we call ourselves believers, we are the most *"unbelieving"* believers I have ever encountered.

Remember what you just read. Your current information is going to fight for its existence, so to have a renewed mind we have to relentlessly read materials that contradict our old ways of thinking. This is how I overcame the poverty mentality. I relentlessly read materials by wealthy people daily. When you read materials about money and success, there is a spirit of wealth or empowerment that comes upon your life. Often you feel energized and excited about your future.

> *Strengthening your mind with wealth information will always be a part of the equation when trying to acquire wealth.*

What happened is that you shifted your brain energy. You told your brain to think another way because the information was positive and it made you feel encouraged -- chemicals in your brain secreted a "happy" or "hopeful" secretion.

Strengthening your mind with wealth information will always be a part of the equation when trying to acquire wealth. Therefore, make sure every day you read something about finance and money.

What you are doing is getting your brain (your mind) accustomed to money, so that money will become your friend and those around you with money will become your friends as well. This is one of the major keys to unlocking your mind to your success potential. It's called tapping into a divine success frequency in your mind.

As you begin fighting to become financially free, let me share with you a synopsis of an article that was written by a lady named Sue Sundstrom about the *"9 Poisonous Thoughts That Hinder Your success."* Sue talked about being a successful business person can be daunting sometimes as well as scary, so if our mindsets are not right about being successful, then we will not succeed. She also encouraged us to watch out for certain thinking patterns that can derail our success. Here is a summary of the nine things she identified that can affect our thinking negatively: (1) I am not good enough; (2) My competition is much better than me, so why would anyone choose my product or service; (3) No matter how hard I try, I will never reach my goal; (4) The task before me is too hard; (5) It's too late, I should have succeeded by now; (6) I am not experience enough, don't have the right knowledge or skill-sets; (7) Success is for others and not me; (8) What will other people think; and (9) There is too much to do, how can I get it all done.

These are great point, so I would like to address these points based on my experience working with my clients, ministry and business partners, family and friends.

(1) I am not good enough

Success really begins in the mind. If you really think you are not good enough or you don't have what it take to make it, you won't. You have to think positive about yourself and believe that you are well able to do whatever you are desiring to do if you want to be successful. Therefore, you cannot think or say – *"you are not good enough."* This type of thinking will always limit you. It is rooted in fear and it will hinder your success. The way to conquer and overcome this thought, is to know that most people are thinking the same thing. You have to learn to do things "afraid." You got to step out beyond your comfort zone and believe for the best no matter what.

(2) My competition is much better than me, so why would anyone choose my product or service

I tell people all the time, there will always be someone doing probably exactly what you are doing, but there is only one of you. If you are truly called to do something in life, there is a segment of the population called to support and finance your purpose. You are unique to your calling and no matter how someone looks like you, they are not you. I like what Sue says about this, competition means that there is a demand for your product or service. You got to know within yourself that you are simply the best like Tina Turner (American pop singer) says in her song, *"Simply the best."* You are better than all the rest, it goes on to say. You got to know that you were anointed for this. You were called to do what you were called to do, and this is your finest hour! Bottom line: You have what people need.

(3) No matter how hard I try, I will never reach my goal

The prize is never given to the one who does not persevere. Persistence and perseverance always beat out talent in the long run. There are a lot of talented people in the world, but there are only a few talented people at the top. What was the difference in some succeeding over others, perseverance? It is true, you can start out with less talent than someone else in your field, but with persistence over time, you can overtake him or her.

(4) The task before me is too hard

Let's face it, reaching your goal in life, will require hard work. You are not going to get around this. But **not** reaching your dream can be even harder especially when you look through the lens of regret and the pain of not enjoying the many joys of life from doing what you were meant to do. Always, remember, you have to be invested in your own dream. Plus, you don't want to be a liability for your own dream and destiny.

(5) It's too late for me; I should have succeeded by now

A winner is someone who has never quit. Never look at your age to determine whether you can do something or not. There are so many people who became successful later on in life. For example; Colonel Sanders, who started Kentucky Fried Chicken. At the age of 65 Colonel Sanders was broke. However, he did not waddle in his bad situation or throw a pity party. Instead, he was determined to succeed in life, and through determination and hard work, an opportunity prevailed for him to sell his fried chicken recipe – and now, making the KFC franchise business a household name. So the key here is not how old you are, but rather how determined you are. Plus, being older can have its perks. Hopefully, you are wiser and you have experienced more in life.

(6) I am not experience enough; don't have the right knowledge or skill-sets

If anyone knows what this feels like is me. Being reared in poverty at the level I was, I had absolutely no skill-sets, knowledge or experience to be successful in life. So no matter who you are and where you came from, we all had to start somewhere. Just focus on being a better you. This is how I started, and I recognized a long time ago there will always be someone better than me. But this did not negate my purpose; what I was called to do. Now, let's flip the switch, there will always be someone who is **NOT** better than you and have **LESS** experience than you. So don't sweat the small stuff, just do your best and stay true to yourself.

I would never have achieved what I have achieved today if I had let this be my excuse. Everything that most children got or received to stimulate them emotionally, intellectually, psychologically, physically, I was an adult, in my mid-twenties, when I received all of this. Again, we are either going to make money or make excuses, but we won't be able to do both. Knowledge is everywhere, just get started and commit your heart to being a lifelong student.

(7) Success is for others and not me

If you are thinking this, there is no way you are going to succeed in any endeavor in life. Successful people come in all shapes and sizes; nationalities and personalities. And for the most part, there is no common denominator except for determination and perseverance. So the question I want to ask you, why not you? If someone else made it in life, so can you!

(8) What will other people think?

I like what New York Times Best-Selling author, Bishop T. D. Jakes says in his book this subject. He said he never saw a hater who was doing better than him. People who are ahead of you will celebrate you and welcome you into the tribe. But for those who have not achieved what you have accomplished or attempting to do, they should not have a voice into your life. Frankly, never listen to people who have never achieved more than you. I like what Sue said in her article about this. She recommends that we remove these types of people out of our equation entirely. And it true, if they are not entrepreneurs themselves, then in all likelihood they will understand very little of what you are going through anyway. You can thank them for their concerns, but don't allow their opinion to weigh in on any decision you might have regarding your success matrix. Please be assured your success as a new entrepreneur hinges on nothing they have to say. You don't need or want their advice because they have never done what you are attempting to do. In this season in your career, only take advice from someone who has done the same thing, **so they can encourage you along the way**. So, '*What will other people think?*' – the answer is: 'Who cares?' Like Sue says, "They are no doubt wonderful people who you enjoy spending time with and care about, but with regard to entrepreneurship, what they think is really not relevant or important to your success."

(9) There is too much to do, how can I get it all done?

The secret of getting ahead is getting started according to author, Mark Twain. Sure, entrepreneurship can be challenging at times, but what goal, dream or vision is not, when attempting to it. Focus is the key here. By focusing on what you need to accomplish, your brain will actually go to work to find solutions for you. This is such a great point. What most people don't know is that the more we ponder on the *"how"* we can accomplish a task, the more our brain will *"expand"* to find solutions to problems. So the primary difference between successful and unsuccessful people is **the way they think**. Therefore, we have to think "right" if we want to be successful.

Every thought that comes to your mind that is negative; I challenge you to challenge it. Know that no matter what, you are well able to succeed and you were made for greatness. Therefore, think high and not low!

Remember, the day that you decide to be wealthy is the day that the universe will come in alignment with your desire!

Step 4

DO WHAT MILLIONAIRES DO

SUCCESS COMES TO THOSE WHO DO AND not to those who just talk. We have to practice principles of success to attract money in our lives. You want to be a millionaire, you want to be wealthy, then you have to do what wealthy people do. While you might not have the money to do or buy everything rich people have, but you can certainly operate in the principles that govern wealth. This is called creating the world you want.

You must be diligent in following principles that create only abundance in your life. We have to practice wealth principles every day when striving to become wealthy.

You must be diligent in following principles that create only abundance in your life. We have to practice wealth principles every day when striving to become wealthy. One of my favorite scriptures in the Bible is Proverbs 10:4, *"The hand of the diligent make rich."* Here is another one I have on my affirmation board, *"Seest thou a man diligent in his business? He shall stand before kings; he shall not stand before mean men,"* (Proverbs 22:29). These scriptures have manifested in my life repeatedly.

For example; one time I found myself on a community program with a former governor of Texas, Governor Rick Perry. He was the governor at that time and when he was coming through my region signing off on a statewide bill, I was asked to be on the program. I can't tell you how nervous I was.

When I arrived the press was everywhere. They seated me on the front row, and one of the television news station reporters asked for my name and who I was with. I remember being so scared giving them my name as I thought to myself, "Please, don't write about me."

When I was asked initially to be on the program, I said, "No way." But my friend kept encouraging me that I could do it. So, eventually, I concurred. I had two to three minutes to share and you better believe it, I called everybody that knew how to get a prayer "through" to pray for me.

I prayed, wrote my two to three minute speech, and rehearsed it repeatedly until I got it down to three minutes. When the moment came for me to

> *Apathy and being overly pessimistic are two major wealth blockage traits. If you are prone to procrastination and being cynical, then people like you have to work extra hard to rid your life of these income reducer traits.*

go on stage to share, my heart was beating so fast though I looked so poised on the outside.

I remember standing in front of the podium adjusting the mic and then beginning my discourse. When I finished, the usher that assisted me off the stage complimented me. When I was seated and looked back up on the stage toward the governor, he gave me a thumb's up. Then after the event, I was asked to oversee a major political party event.

Proverbs 22:29 came alive in my life this day. I had been diligent in pursuing my passion and doing what wealthy people do, so I began to reap the benefit of being consistent and relentless – *it brought me before great people!*

Apathy and being overly pessimistic are two major wealth blockage traits. If you are prone to procrastination and being cynical, then people like you have to work extra hard to rid your life of these income reducer traits. These traits will always talk you out and hinder you from receiving greatness in your life.

For me, these are the type of people as well overall negative people, I try to keep my distance from. Because I am such a positive and forward thinker, I don't have time to try and justify every thought, action and decision I made based on "what if." I have a strong dislike of people who try to talk me out of my destiny. I like people who talk my destiny "up" and not "down."

It is hard enough to do things afraid, so you want to position yourself everyday with benchmarks that will provoke you to keep doing or pressing towards your destiny. Also, keep in mind, you will be doing intentional things that will be going against your comfort zone, so you have to be highly motivated in this stage in your wealth journey.

Remember, it is about *practicing* wealth principles. Therefore, you want

> *It is hard enough to do things afraid, so you want to position yourself everyday with benchmarks that will provoke you to keep doing or pressing towards your destiny.*

to challenge your thoughts, your motives, your ideas, your understanding, your personal biases, anything that has brought you to the conclusion or resolve that you have about something. The reason this is important, because these are the reasons, concepts, and proclivities that can cause you to make a decision to do a certain thing or act at any given time. What is your goal – *to do what wealthy people do?*

It is said that we are a creature of habits, so if you are desiring to create new habits, then make sure you are conscious of your "world" and that your cues in your mind or benchmarks would remind you that you are operating out of your old self – your broke mentality.

For example: If you are accustomed to saying when facing hardship or challenges, "Lord, if it ain't one thing; it's another." Then you want to set up markers in your spirit that would repel this saying. What do I mean? You want to make, "ain't" or "can't" your marker words.

So on a large piece a paper, write the words, "ain't" or "can't." Then while looking at these words, you say to "ain't" and "can't" out loud you are not a part of my wealth language or my destiny. Repeat this over and over again out loud for about 5 minutes three to five time a day. Now, if you want to go deeper with this, you can record yourself on your cell phone telling yourself that these words are not a part of your wealth life.

Activate, activate, activate is the only way things are going to get done or stimulated. Even water just sitting still gets stale...Whatever you are learning about being wealthy and financially free, you got to start doing **immediately.**

Yes, I know, "ain't" is not correct grammar, but the reality is, most of us use colloquial and slang language daily to communicate.

Don't get so caught up on the technical stuff or being politically correct, just master the exercise and watch your mind eventually naturally reject those words. You want your brain to be in an autopilot state when it comes to these words.

Activate, activate, activate is the only way things are going to get done or stimulated. Even water just sitting still gets stale. And if it sits long enough; a foul odor will begin to waft from it. So whatever you are learning about being wealthy and financially free, you got to start doing *immediately.*

Don't wait for tomorrow, find something you can do now. It does not matter how small it is, do something different toward your wealth destiny NOW! Again, it is not in the saying; it is in the doing!

Rich people
don't set limits for
what they can have;
Poor people focus
on what they don't
have.

Step 5

PROVOKE
DIVINE
INTELLIGENCE

ANOTHER THING YOU WANT TO DO when you begin changing or shifting your mindset is that you want to provoke divine intelligence into your situation. You want to activate the power that is within prayer.

Prayer and meditation have been used for centuries by almost every religion to bring solace to our hearts, minds and souls. But one of the other byproducts of prayer, is that you are able to connect with your inner man – your true self. You hear things from the "invisible" world that often bring enlightenment to many things and areas in our lives. If you are not one that prays and meditate, let me encourage you to start today. It will revolutionize your life.

The world is a very noisy and busy place. In order for us to hear what we never heard before, often we have to get somewhere quiet and meditate.

The world is a very noisy and busy place. In order for us to hear what we never heard before, often we have to get somewhere quiet and meditate. I wrote a book called, *"Pray & Grow Richer,"* it is for me an anthology of how I soaked in the presence of God for wealth and increase and it manifested. I made an intentional demand on the wealth that was locked up inside of me to come forth – to show itself, to manifest! In four years, it manifested in a tremendous way in my life. Now, almost seven years later, all of my wealth coaches are millionaires.

Joshua 1:8 says in the Bible, *"meditate in the word of God, we will have good success."* When we meditate and become quiet soaking and basking in the presence of God, we open up our minds and spirits to hear things we never heard or seen before.

As I laid out on the floor in the wee hours of the mornings, with soaking music on, ideas and creative ventures began to bombard my mind. I would see all types of opportunities to create multi-streams of income. From packaging to promotional ideas to product development to pricing adjustments. Every service we offered in our consultant group, I began to think differently about them.

I even learned how to manage my time more and how to delegate more effectively. Everything and everyone I practically needed came into my equation and it is still happening. I heard of so many of my counterparts working so hard to network and meet certain influential individuals. For me, when I "networked" with God on the floor, all these people came into my equation. So I did not have to run around to every luncheon and event to meet people. I am truly grateful for this! This is a lesson I have made a part of my life. Bottom line: The closer you become to the creative presence and power within you, the closer you come to the success frequency of the universe.

Lastly, when you provoke divine intelligence into your situation, another spiritual realm will be stirred up or activated and that is – dream cycles. You will find yourself dreaming more purposeful things. Instead of randomly meaningless thoughts and events, your dreams will depict what you are trying to achieve when you are awake. I just saw this statement on one of my social media outlets, *"Always remember to fall asleep with a dream and wake up with a purpose."* Some dreams will give you insight into your future destiny. I talk about this more in my book, *"The Midnight Cry."*

This was so amazing to me. I was always a dreamer. I guess it was an inherited trait, because my mother was a dreamer as well. She was always having dreams about events and our family members when we were growing up. For her and me, our dreams required no interpretation. They were literal per se. What and who we dreamt about, it was truly about them or it.

Many times my mother would know about car accidents and crisis before they happened. She would also have dreams about family members when they were pregnant. She would be led to do things and go places by dreams. When she told us about these occurrences, she said she would say, "Lord, what do You want me to see or go." For a child growing up hearing these stories, it was exciting!

When my brothers were getting in trouble and fights hanging out in clubs and bad neighborhoods, it was normal for her to have a dream weeks before they got into trouble. She would ask God to watch over them and spare their lives. And as she saw in a dream that is exactly what happened.

So many of my mother's dreams were fascinating. Things probably many people would not believe. But growing up in her home, I know these things to be true. Just let me say this, it was hard to get away with mischief growing up in her household.

But let me get back to what I was talking about. Probably the best way to confirm this is that our consultant group, *Clark's Consultant Group*, was birthed out of a dream. We were already in business, but it was in a dream that I saw so many more business and financial opportunities that we had not taken advantage of. From that dream, our business offerings expanded, our client base increased and, of course, our income went up. I believe strongly in the power of prayer, meditation and basking in the presence of God. If you want to know more about dreams and visions and how to activate this aspect of prayer more in your life, please visit our institute website at: www.anointedforbusiness.org and enroll in our dreams and visions school. This is a biblical study of dreams and visions in the Bible and how dreams and visions were oftentimes used to show us our destiny. It is not about being "spooky" or anything crazy, but a systematic scientific training in this topical subject. When you complete this school, you will receive a certificate of completion. Go ahead, check it out!

But the reason prayer and meditation work when it comes down to success and prosperity is because when we quiet our souls from the noise of

> *The reason prayer works when it comes down to success and prosperity is because when we quiet our souls from the noise of this world, we can then tap into our God-given abilities and talents.*

this world, we can then tap into our God-given abilities and talents, which ultimately allows us to tap into our success frequency. I am truly convinced that most of us are marred and that we are doing things in life (working on jobs we hate, in college in majors we don't like, etc.) that is not what we have been called to do. I heard this year, *a career is what we pay for; a calling is what we are made for.* We only live once, so I encourage you to be courageous and live life according to your life's purpose and destiny.

Well, Dr. Clark, I don't know my life's purpose or destiny? If this is you, then I encourage you to soak and meditate everyday aggressively. You have to be intentional about following your dreams and destiny in life. No one is going to pursue your personal dreams harder than you. You got to become an advocate for your dreams and destiny to come to pass.

You got to fight and claw your way against voices and invisible forces in this world that want to keep you poor and broke. It's alright to be different and to have your own rhythm. The prize is never given to similarities; it is always given to the ones who are extraordinary or above the crowd.

Here are some benchmarks you should know if you are believing for success and prosperity to happen in your life:

- You have to have a vision for the top

- You have to see increase not decrease

- You have to have a vision for the whole and not just for the part

- You have to put a picture on the canvas of your mind where you want to go

- You must understand that the power of God stops where your imagination stops

- You have to accept the assignment, then agree with the alignment

- You must believe, you cannot fail

- You have to constantly update yourself, so you won't be outdated

- You can't make a difference, if you are not different

- You have to embrace change or you will become a museum – reminiscing only on things that happened in the past.

- You can't stand out, if you won't step out

- You have to live life for tomorrow and not for today because what you do today will determine your tomorrow

- You are not made to conform, but to be transformed

- You must strive to be your own person because the desire to be like everybody else is the reason we have too many nobodies.

- You can't be in the middle of the road and not be ran over

- You have to take control of your life or your life will control you

- You can't expect change if you don't change

- You can't be an overcomer if you don't have something to overcome

- You can't be a leader when you are always looking to others to lead you

- You must think big to get big things

- You have to think wealth and not poverty

- You can't manifest if you don't show up

- You have to defeat fear in your life, otherwise, fear will debilitate you in life

- You have to know you will never achieve greatness in your life if you never conceive it

- You have to know that you are blessed and not curse

- You have to know you were born to do great things and not small things

- You are a winner and not a quitter

Rich people create their financial world; Poor people depend on others to do it for them.

Step 6

ASSOCIATE WITH WEALTHY PEOPLE

WE ALL NEED MENTORS, COACHES and sponsors when trying to pursue our next level of wealth. Associating with wealthy people or people who are financially free is a great segue to you becoming wealthy. It is amazing to me that as I engage more and more with wealthy people how much information and resources are available that I did not know about until I met them. This is such a huge wonderful component to interfacing with people with money. Now, when I am in the presence of the wealthy; I am always mindful that new insights and revelations are ever-present for me to draw from.

I like what Kenneth Brown says in his book, _"LIFE: Six Principles for Successful Living."_ "You can't be what you can't see, so you need to hang around people who will set you on fire, not douse you with cold water. You need to hang around people who will edify you, who are going to tell you that anything's possible." When you have dreams, he says, you have to protect them.

> *Success is not achieve just through luck, intelligence or education, but rather where you spend your time and who you spend your time with.*

Success is not achieve just through luck, intelligence or education, but rather where you spend your time and who you spend your time with. Time spent with empowerment people is time well spent. This is why I love spending time with my millionaire girlfriend, Yvette Munroe. Every time I am with her, she brings clarity and insight into my life. So much value comes to my life when I spend time with her and her husband. They are such great people.

I remember last year when I was spending a few days in their home that one morning when I came downstairs I saw her husband at the computer adjacent to the kitchen and den.

As I passed by him, I noticed he was on a website that looked like a bookstore. He was looking around and because I am in the book publishing business, I became curious. I said to him, "What are you doing over here. What is this?" He said, "I am downloading audiobooks for me to listen to in the car." "Taken back," "I said really? Show me what you're talking about." As he began to show me what the website had to offer and to let me listen to some samples of the audiobooks, "a bell went off in my head." And I said out loud, "We can do this! We can offer this service! My husband is going to read these books and we are going to offer this service now when I get back home. We just added more income into our promotional contract."

Armed with this newfound information and insight, I came back saying with everything inside of me that we are going to do this as a business. We were going to offer this service. I told my husband about it, and I said, "Baby, if you can do this, this can bring an additional thousands of dollars for our marketing and publishing contracts." He somewhat said yes, but I knew no matter what he said; it was going to happen.

Well, within a matter of weeks; it came to pass. Not sure how all of it unfolded, but I was on the phone with a covenant partner, and all of a sudden he began to talk about the distribution service they utilize for their publishing consultant business. That's right, you guessed it. They offered audiobook service. When he told me this; I knew this was the window of opportunity we were looking for. So he initiated a call with the owner, and now our Writer's Agency, Jabez Books, offers audiobook service. But the beauty of this new relationship not only allowed us to offer audiobooks, but it afforded us with a larger base for global distribution, as well as we are now able to offer book translation into three languages: Spanish, French and Chinese.

This is what interfacing with the rich and famous will open your life up to – more insight, more revelation, more information, more favor, more resources, and more money. The fringe benefits are endless when we spend time with high energy money making individuals.

You have a right to select who you want to spend your personal space with. If this is so, if I was you, and I am believing to be financially free, then I would do everything in my power and energy to spend it with people with influence and wealth.

If you are a dreamer and your dream is big, you will never achieve your dream in life spending time only with people with small dreams or people who have *only* experienced small dreams.

You see, possibilities are products of your perspective.

Hanging around rich and wealthy people, will expand your horizon. They will cause you to dream.

Becoming wealthy is not *a matter of an accident, but a matter of attraction.*

> *Possibilities are products of your perspective. Hanging around rich and wealthy people, will expand your horizon. They will cause you to dream. Becoming wealthy is not a matter of an accident, but a matter of attraction.*

The law of attraction says, we will attract that which is within us. As we associate with more wealthy people, wealth will become more of an internal innate magnet inside of us. Everywhere you go, people of means will be drawn to you.

For example; this year (2015), I had the privilege to be a part of the Author's Pavilion for the National Congressional Black Caucus. I was thrilled to have been selected to do a book signing there with my latest book, *"Think Like A Millionaire, Be A Millionaire."* However, I was even more elated when I received an email two days before the event that shared with me that I had also been selected to be a panel guest regarding the topic, "The African American family and wealth." What an honored I thought. Plus, President Barack Obama was scheduled to speak at this event a few days later, and here I am now, being asked to be a panel guest in the Author's Pavilion. Whoaaaaaa!!!!

When I woke up that morning preparing to go to the airport to catch the plane from Texas to Washington, DC; I was so excited. The panel discussion was scheduled for 2 p.m. to 3 p.m., on a Thursday afternoon and knowing that I was going to lose an hour going to the East coast from the West Coast, I wanted to make sure I arrived in DC way ahead of time. My flight landed about 10:50 a.m., so I knew I should have enough time to get there early to set up and be prepared for the panel.

Thank God, I did arrive when I did. Because that day was 9/11 and all the rental cars were in use at the rental car company I rented a car from. Everyone had to wait about an hour to get a rental car. As rental cars were being returned, those were the cars that were being rented to us. So we had to wait for them to wash and clean each car.

When it was 12 p.m., I could feel my body beginning to tense, but I would immensely fight against it mentally. Shortly after 12 p.m., I was in a car heading towards the Washington Convention. I intentionally worked hard to stay in a relaxed state. I was a little apprehensive about this whole experience because it had been years that I drove in DC and I remembered it was not a pretty picture back then. If anything I knew, parking might be a problem also. So mentally, I was calmly factoring in all of this in regards to arriving to my destination on time.

As I thought, parking was a slight problem, but I decided to ask an attendant where to park. He instructed me where to go and I parked securely in a parking garage, and I took plenty of pictures of the car and where I parked to make sure I knew how to get back.

Once I did this, I rushed to the convention center, found where I was supposed to go and was set up by 1:30 p.m. When it was time for our panel discussion, I wanted to be ready, rested and focused. Thank God, the panel discussion time was pushed back, so I was able to regroup a little bit longer.

When the panel discussion began, we were all asked to share our philosophy about money and the African American community. We had a panel of four and each was from a different background. One was a former Vice-President of a university. Another one was a very young lady who had written a book on finance and how to get out of debt, I believe. And the other one was a young man from Tennessee who owned apartment complexes and a few office buildings.

As each of us shared our philosophy about money, I recognized early on that my concept about wealth and being financially free mirrored what the young man believed. I really loved the fact that he was so young and owned what he did.

The other panelists dealt with money, wealth and finance based on the traditional teaching and understanding of money. While they were not wrong in what they were sharing per se, myself and the other young man addressed these issues based on the premise for the need for people to become entrepreneurs, so that they could create their own world, strive toward becoming financially free.

When it was time for me to share my philosophy about money, I quoted Ecclesiastes 9:16, first to start off my dialogue. I told them that this verse says, *"...a poor man's wisdom is despised, and nobody wants to hear him."* I told them my philosophy about money is that we have got to have our own stuff. We have to own businesses, become an entrepreneur; we have to create our own world. I said, as long as we are broke, nobody want to hear us. As long as we are broke, we have no sphere of influence. So we have to get off the menu (wanting for someone to give us something) and have a seat at the table. I went on to say, we got to think like employers and not employees. So my philosophy is that we have got to do a better job in raising up entrepreneurs, a society who can take care of themselves, and this is what I am called to do — raise up entrepreneurs (and as we say in the faith community, kingdompreneurs).

As the panel discussion continued, I was also abled to address the traditional thought concerning education giving the African American person access to better jobs and opportunities. While I did not disagree with this, but I wanted to bring clarity to what the word, "access" really meant.

I pointed out the fact that the word "access" that we so often get after being educated is what puts us in debt for the most part. Yes, we get better jobs and have more opportunities, I said to the audience, but *most* educational systems teach us how to become employees instead of employers. They teach us to make someone else rich, and not you. I continued to share in more details what the word access entailed– more consumer debt, more car payments, more mortgages, and more school loans, which are all controlled by someone else -- the lending system.

In addition, I shared that we cannot depend on anyone else or corporate America to make us rich because if this was true, more people would retire rich and not broke. So let's face the fact, we got to teach people how to own their own businesses or become an entrepreneur because the systems of this world generate offspring of poor broke retirees.

At the end of the panel, quite a few people began to come to me. The first person that introduced himself to me was a man named George Fraser. He said I agreed with you and understood everything you said. I had never met Georg Fraser before, so I did not know him when I saw him. However, I had just heard about him a few months prior. If you don't know George Fraser, let me encourage you to look him up on the internet.

But just to share a little bit about him. Mr. Fraser is an incredible entrepreneur who hosts one of the nation's larger power networking conference annually. Thousands of people attend his conference and he has a network called, "Frasernet," which is my understanding has a huge number of members. So I was encouraged and thrilled to hear him say this to me when I found out who he was.

Another lady that was in the audience also approached me after the panel discussion and literally sat me down and talked with me for at least 30 minutes after the session. She shared with me that she was a business owner and she owned a security company with 500 employees.

As well, two other ladies introduced themselves to me and they told me they were the head or President of a Chamber of Commerce in New York and they would love for me to come and speak at their chamber some time. I told them, I would be honored, just let me know the date as soon as possible.

There were others that shared how they were blessed by what I said, and shared with me about their businesses, but the reason I shared all of this is to say, the people in the room that had wealth, were business owners, and were entrepreneurs are the ones that were attracted to me. Now, I am not saying, I was that important, but the point I am making is that like beget like. Because I

We live in a voice activation system. What you put out in the universe will come back to you.... Whatever you are, you attract.

understood their world or spoke at the level of their understanding, they embraced me and brought me into their "world."

We live in a voice activation system. What you put out in the universe will come back to you. Business people, authors, writers, entrepreneurs, speakers, religious leaders, civic officials, prayer leaders, media, and entertainment industry people will always be attracted to me because these entities are components of my life. It is the same with you. Whatever you are, you attract. So if you are attracting the wrong type of people in your life consistently, then there is an aroma or fragrance coming from your life that draws these types of individuals that you need to change.

When I started my journey toward becoming wealthy, I wanted to be mentored by millionaires. At that time, I had four millionaires in my life. None of them were accessible on a regular basis, at least not at the level I would need in order to be mentored properly. Sure, I could call three of them from time to time to get some counselling, but that was sporadic. Now, I have access to six multi-millionaires, and five of them this year (2015), toured with me. I will be forever grateful.

My mind has been expanded as well as my spirit. To have people at this level of wealth to embrace me and believe in me is pretty incredible. Just recently I realized this is not the norm for most people. Sometimes when things happen to you, you just kind of process it as being normal. But I just came to grip with the fact, this is not the norm for persons who are not millionaires. Then how did this happen for me? I changed what was "in" my mind.

I talked about it in chapter three that you have to learn how to think like a millionaire. What I did, I filled my mind with **ONLY** millionaires' thoughts, knowledge, principles, understanding, so while my bank account did not look like a millionaire, my mind and my understanding operated from a millionaire mentality. So much so that it drew millionaire into my life.

I dare you to try it. Listen, do what I did. Go to the library and check out books *only* by millionaires and read them for the next 90 days. You can also buy books on Amazon that were written by millionaires as well. The key here is to only read books by millionaires. There are a lot books written on money and finance, but the people writing them are not millionaires.

You see, a financial analyst can write on finances, but it does not make him a millionaire. Why is this important? There is a wealth spirit attached to wealth, and when you read materials that are written by wealthy people that spirit engulfs your life. This is what I saw happen in my life. And it happened repeatedly.

Some books as I read them, I felt like things literally were shifted inside of me like gears shifting on a factory machine. This really made an impact in and on my life. This is why I am so passionate about helping others. Yes, I know everyone is not going to follow through, but somebody will. I am more focused on the "somebody will" than those who will not. The dominant thought(s) in your mind is what is going to be drawn into your life. I think success not defeat.

I heard once that when the Canadian American actor, Jim Carrey, was just beginning his career as an actor that he declared that everybody wanted to work with him. As the story goes; he went up on an elevated place in his city and declared over the city that everybody wanted to work with him. And, it is my understanding that it wasn't too long after this; that people in the entertainment industry began coming into his life, and they wanted to work with him.

Jim also believed strongly in the law of attraction. It is reported that during an interview with Oprah Winfrey in 1997, he revealed that as a struggling actor, he would visualize himself receiving a check for $10,000,000 for his acting career. Well, seven years later, Jim received a check for $10,000,000 for his role in the *Dumb and Dumber* movie.

What did Jim do? What he conceived in his mind, he believed he could do it. Then he spoke it and it came to pass. Today, he is described as one of the most famous and biggest comedic actors in Hollywood.

Just recently, a young man by the name of Kevin Caldwell released an ebook titled, *"Rich Friends, Broke Friends: How are your friends influencing your money?"* When I saw it being advertised on Facebook, I immediately bought it and read it.

It was a cute little ebook that outlined a few comparative traits of rich friends versus poor friends. It was broken down into two parts: Rich People Traits and Poor People Traits. Here are the things he identified in his book for each category:

Rich Friends' Traits:

- ❖ Rich friends pay themselves first
- ❖ Rich friends have a millionaire mentor
- ❖ Rich friends learn every tax angle they can
- ❖ Rich friends work smarter
- ❖ Rich friends stay balanced

Poor Friends' Traits:

- ❖ Poor friends pay bills first
- ❖ Poor friends learn money tips from middle class friends
- ❖ Poor friends anticipate tax refund
- ❖ Poor friends let emotions rule financial decisions
- ❖ Poor friends pay interest instead of earning interest

If you have not read this book, let me encourage you to purchase it. While most of the information was not new to me, but all the stories in each chapter were. Sometimes it is not about whether you heard something or not, but it is the *"new"* information in the midst of the old that just might be what you need for your breakthrough. Great job, Kevin!

The Make or Break List

I also read another interesting article on the internet about "The Make or Break List." It was about how the people you surround yourself with can either make or break your success. It said if you want to be amazing, then you have to surround yourself with amazing people.

In this article it talks about a man who brought himself up from rags to riches. It says that this man was living from paycheck to paycheck, but one day he got tired of being broke. So the first thing he did he looked at his friends. Most of his friends looked like him – struggling and barely making it, but there was one person he looked at that wasn't particularly smart or more talented, but he was quite wealthy. He asked the man how he became wealthy. How did he became a millionaire? The wealthy man's response was simple: **"keep the right company."**

The article say this man took this advice to heart, then he assessed his current friends. He realized most of his friends had no desire to do better, so he sought out to find some new friends.

It is said that he went around to conventions and seminars to connect with people who had made something of themselves. After this, he replaced all the people in his network, then he made a list. It was a two column list. In one column, he listed all the people who would improve his life, and in the other column, he listed the people who would drag him down.

"If someone could improve his life, he spent as much time around them as possible. If someone could possibly drag him down, he never spent more than *five minutes* around them. After following his "make or break" list, the man was able to become a millionaire within *three years,"* according to the writer. Wow, what a powerful story!

Another way to streamline or rid your life of people that might hinder your success is to go through your contact list on your cell phone. Put each person in your contact list on the **keep** or **delete** list. By using the same criteria from the make or break list, streamline your contact list. I read once there are only three essential persons you must have in your life to succeed:

1. A person who is older and more successful than you to learn from

2. A person who is equal to you to exchange ideas with

3. A person below you to coach and keep you energized

"Every great person was, is, or will be successful because of the company he or she keeps. They will make an impact because of a successful network of driven peers who provide both inspiration and healthy competition. If you want to be remarkable, you must constantly challenge and surround yourself with remarkable people. So think about what your goals are, and take a look around you. Do you need to write a "make or break" list?" This writer says.

- ❖ If you hang around five confident people, you will be the sixth.
- ❖ If you hang around five intelligent people, you will be the sixth.
- ❖ If you hang around five millionaires, you will be the sixth.
- ❖ If you hang around five idiots, you will be the sixth.
- ❖ If you hang around five broke people, you will be the sixth.
- ❖ It's inevitable

— Peter Voogd

Rich people have winning attitudes; Poor people have defeated aptitudes

Step 7

ESTABLISH A BUSINESS

One of the surest ways to die broke is to retire from a job after working there for 25 years or more without any other stream of income. Of course, there are always exceptions, but only 5% of people out of a 100 people retire financially free after working 20 years or more. There is nothing sadder to me than to see senior citizens working trying to make a living **after** they have retired. My heart goes out to everyone I see in this predicament. Listen, having a job is honorable, but it is like trying to win the lottery if you think you are going to retire and be rich or financially free.

Let me encourage you to consider entrepreneurship. There are so many opportunities available to you because of the internet. Our Marketing Director, Melanie Bonita, made $20,000 in one year just selling products and services on Instagram. Sure, it can be scary, but

Having a job is honorable, but it is like trying to win the lottery if you think you are going to retire and be rich or financially free.

> *No one is going to create your world for you, and you should not or cannot depend on corporate America to do this for you as well. The only person you can depend on that is going to show up every time is yourself.*

there is too much information available on the internet to guide you through these unsure moments.

The thing I want to stress in this section is that no one is going to create your world for you and you should not or cannot depend on corporate America to do this for you. The only person you can depend on that is going to show up every time is *yourself.* So let's get some backbone, assess your skill-sets and prepare your heart and mind to be an entrepreneur or business owner.

Now, I know for many, one of the biggest challenge might be, how am I going to raise the money or capital to start a business? If this is you, I read a wonderful article on the internet written by Jonathan Long (Founder & CEO, Market Dominion Media) that was about this topic that I would like to glean from to answer this question. The article was title, *"8 Musts to Start Your Business With Little to No Capital."* To read the full article ‰ http://www.entrepreneur.com/article/‸ really recommend that you read it

Here are the eight tips he outlined that can help you get your idea off the ground with limited funds.

1. **Build your business around what you know.** Stick with what you know when you are building your business. By doing this, you can eliminate the need to hire consultants and other people with skill-sets that you don't have. Sometimes it is just having the knowledge is all you need to be successful.

2. **Tell everyone you know what you are doing.** When starting a business tell everyone you know: family, friends, business associates and past colleagues, etc. Send out emails, call some of your closest friends and family members to get their buy in and don't forget to share it on all the social networks (Facebook, Twitter, Google Plus, Instagram, YouTube, LinkedIn, etc.).

3. **Avoid unnecessary expenses.** There are so much free stuff given out on the internet (postcards, business cards, trial programs, stationeries, websites, etc.), so

before you start paying for some basic office supplies, equipment or service, check on the internet first to see if someone or a company is offering them free. You want to avoid spending money on your start up business as much as possible. Being frugal in the beginning can be the difference between a successful and a failed business.

4. **Don't get buried in credit card debt.** I know in the past many new entrepreneurs and business owners were told to take out a business credit card and pay for all of your office equipment on it.

But what many have found out now, this was a suicidal way to use credit when starting a business. Today, it is recommended that you use your company's revenue to finance your expenses. Eliminating the stress and burden of debt will greatly increase the chances of you creating a successful business.

Also, when I needed new office computer equipment, I used the Home Shopping Network (www.hsn.com) to acquire what I needed. What they do is send you what you need immediately, but you are put on a payment plan for a certain amount of month. Automatically, each month (whether it is 3 to 6 months) they will debit it from your bank account. I got all the office equipment (tablet, camera, and laptop) that I needed in six months without running up any credit card debit.

5. **Make sure your receivables policy won't sink you.** If you are offering consulting or products to retailers, you want to create a payout payment plan that is beneficial to you. In other words, you want to make sure you can remain above water if you have a payout net-15 or net-30 terms. Jonathan recommends that we not base

our receivables on what we think our customers will want. He says we should base them on what is going to make our business operate successfully.

6. **Build up sweat equity.** Starting a business from scratch will always require sweat equity. Expect to work long hours because it takes a while to build your brand and business, but it is worth it in the long run. As it is said, "Rome was not built in a day," so don't expect your business to be built in a day. Go ahead work long hours; you are worth it and your business is worth it.

7. **Take advantage of free advertising and marketing.** You don't have to break your bank to promote and market your business. You can generate a buzz around what you do using social media outlets. Social media is great for this. Facebook has $5 promotional opportunities to promote your post and website to any target audience to get leads and potential clients. I use this service all the time. We have met and learned about some businesses, organizations, people, and services that we needed. There are also opportunities to promote your website. You want to take advantage of these websites

features. So many people, businesses, and organizations have reached out to me because of social media marketing.

8. **Get ready to hustle.** Hard work and dedication is a must for new start up business owners and entrepreneurs. The bottom line: little capital to work with, then the more you would have to work the business. So you are the CEO, Operational Manager, Administrative Assistant, Accountant, Sale Manager, Customer Service Support and everything else your business needs require. But don't let having a limited capital prevent

you from taking a great idea and running with it. The race is not given to the swift, but to the person that endures to the end.

You have what it takes to make it. If you don't have a business start one today. Assess your skill-sets, prepare the correct documents (flyers, brochures, business cards, postcards, etc.); and start telling everybody about it.

Next, design a workshop, seminar or webinar around your business. Don't forget to collaborate. Collaborative endeavors are big these days. Connect with others in your region that compliment what you are doing and create a program together.

You have to start somewhere, and this is a great way to start. Here is the golden rule: If you have a little sphere of influence, then you want to connect or do endeavors with people who have a larger sphere of influence than you. The key here is that you have to bring something to the table that will engage or encourage these types of people to partner with you.

For years, I was always asked to do this or do that. At first, I thought it was about my skill-sets, but as I grew older and wiser, I learned it was about my sphere of influence and network. I remember being invited to a private prayer breakfast with a former governor of Texas. When the meeting was over, the lady who invited me said, *"Do you know why you were invited? I said, "No."* She said, *"They wanted to invite people to this meeting that had networks or great following."* I said, *"Okay,"* and went on mingling.

Did this discourage me, no! I was not discouraged at all because the reality is, if we are going to get ahead, we have to at some point in our lives rely on other people's influence to get us into the room. However, it is up to us to stay in the room.

I can't thank God enough for the people who have believed and supported me that were ahead of me. They embraced me and gave me strength to keep pressing on. I sincerely thank all of them from the bottom of my heart. We all need a few people above and ahead of us to believe in us. So be courageous, start the business now!

Luke 19:13 says:

*So he called ten of his servants, and gave them ten minas [one apiece, each equal to about a hundred days' wages] and said to them, '**Do business [with this] until I return.'** (AMP)*

*Calling ten of his servants, he gave them ten minas, and said to them, '**Engage in business until I come.'** (ESV)*

So he called ten of his servants together. He gave a bag of money to each servant. He said, '***Do business with this money until I come back.'*** (ERV)

Rich people own businesses; poor people own things

Step 8

SOW UP

FOR THE MOST PART, MILLIONAIRES ARE generous people. As your income increase, you got to sow UP! Meaning, your giving cannot be at the level it used to be at. You have to sow at the measure you are being or have been blessed.

Take a lesson from billionaires, Bill Gates, Warren Buffett, Ken Langore, Oprah Winfrey and Carl Icahn. These men give millions of dollars to charities, universities and medical research institutions. You can never get away from giving when you are blessed with so much.

> *Giving is always the flip side of success. When you make it, you have to become an advocate for other people's success.*

Giving is always the flip side of success. When you make it, you have to become an advocate for other people's success. Life is truly about give and take. As I have received more, I have sown more.

We have to sow up if we want the floodgates of wealth to continually be opened over our lives. And particularly, for those of us who call ourselves Christians. The Bible says, God will give us power to get wealth, so that His covenant might be established throughout the earth. What does this means? We are to be the light and to be caregivers to the world. One of our main purposes for accumulation is distribution. We should never forget this when acquiring wealth.

> *When my income when up, I sow up.*

When my income when up, I sow up. I look to giving more and more as I continue this wealth journey. I am so looking forward to the moment where I can finance entire missionary trips and community endeavors.

This particular book is a part of a community endeavor that I just launched in my children's name (Danielle & Quinton Clark): **The BLESSED Society**. It is a foundation that will assist children with

Everything I do going forward will be about paying it forward. I have been so wonderfully blessed that I want to make sure others make it as well. While I am not a billionaire yet, but I am capable of becoming a billionaire.

learning, reading and writing disabilities within the established educational system based on my childhood experience. For every *"BLESSED"* book that is sold, we are going to set 10% aside to assist children in the community.

Everything I do going forward will be about paying it forward. I have been so wonderfully blessed that I want to make sure others make it as well. While I am not a billionaire yet, but I am capable of becoming a billionaire. But no matter where I am at in my financial situation, I will continue to *sow up,* so I can continue to *grow up* financially. Let me encourage you to do the same.

Have a great life and I will see you at the **TOP – T**he **O**utstanding **P**erson you are.

In conclusion: we will always have seed when we sow – *"And [God] Who provides **seed for the sower** and bread for eating **will also provide and multiply your [resources for] sowing and increase the fruits of your righteousness** [which manifests itself in active goodness, kindness, and charity]," (2 Corinthians 9:10 Amplified Version).*

Rich people give freely; poor people complain about giving

Please visit Dr. Clark's website

to purchase more of her products:

www.drshirleyclark.org
1-877-356-4711

Pray & Grow Richer Book Set

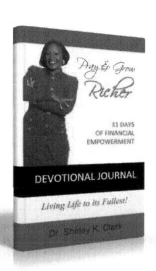

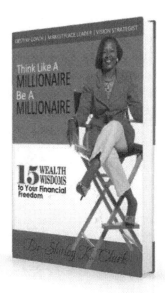

Purpose & Destiny
Series

Made in the USA
Columbia, SC
26 December 2017